wingspeak

by ioana gheorghiu

wingspeak

ISBN: 9798809744942

This book is for those who want nothing more than freedom, seek nothing else but peace, and serve nothing less than love itself.

What you seek is seeking you.

~ Rumi

contents

this
is wingspeak.
look not to these words,
but to what they are pointing to.
oceanwards. skyleaning growth. but only with
burrowfeet, sturdy anchors, indestructible pillars:
i am powerful
i am gifted
i am beautiful
i am in the right place
at the right time.
now go. carry on.

language is not an arrival, an endpoint —
use it more like an arrow. aim your bow
at the tao that cannot be named. cross spaces with it.
build bridges. awaken the sacredness.
do not confuse it for the sacred.

language only leads to the edge of consciousness.
beyond that, it is your leapweight that matters.
your featherbound will. your bravecall.

ayoooo ahewa yii

when you arrive
in the sky that you are,
come back to the land.
show others the way.
wingspeak.

follow your soul dreams

this was seed and sparkle and serenade. the dream you held, curled inside apostrophes to sleep, popping up in a conversation here and there. we are all born with one, you know. it coils inside its own longing, undisturbed. you had no way of knowing, darling, that a dream like that goes unacknowledged your whole life. like a sleeping dragon, you notice it now and then by the rising and falling of its breathing chest.

it doesn't wake in the noise nor in the spotlight. a dragon wakes when you look away for a moment, distracted by something small and beautiful and free. it wakes when your desperation and need of having it gone humbles itself into acceptance that it's there. god, it's still there. it wakes when you no longer want to drive it out and replace it by something a little less fantastic. something with a little less weight. just please give me something with a little less potential for bringing my whole life down in flames.

but dreams are dangerous, darling.

and you were built for them. your vision of the world and you inside it. finally, you inside it — looking out, looking through, belonging. arriving home. arriving you. because you're the only one who knows that in the wake of the flames, only the unneeded burns. and whatever's left is all that was really yours anyway. so let your chest fill and flame and flounder in the mystery of what's yet to come. in the fantastical realm of dream into matter. in the courage to chase what elevates and leave what weighs. your dragon knows the way. go. go to the edge of wherever it leads. and never look back.

WHAT IS REAL

what is real
but the pull to go on

we need you here
reel in
your un-destruction
wise peeled & shameless
speaking from your bareness
what we know is ageless
what we know is howled at
scorned at
frowned at
bowed at
when we have crossed beyond the markings
felt beneath the tide
drowned out & came out
carrying secrets

wish your undoing
and in time, these lyrical hands
will turn each cave inside out
mine the wonders
the giants will be holding

this is a place to talk to you
this is no place to talk to you
the ethers are moving
are we?
are we
inside
what
is real

THIRST

tea kettle whistling, i finish
a message
to you
while re-evaluating my relation
ship with time
and what it means to
slow-simmer your dreams
but the tea is imminent
and behind me, through blinds
i watch clouds gathering
preparing to burst
and rain is imminent
while the dog is pawing at the door,
a painting falls off the wall
into the hands of imminent
gravity
and i still need to meditate

before the house gets loud
my soul is imminent
my timing
my calling
my voice
inside of me
LOUD
my inklings my wordings my smoke and fire
HOT
urgent
pleading
like the whistling of the kettle
loud louder loudest
i am becoming steam evaporating
into the dark skies

raining down on the valley
quenching the thirst
it too
was very
imminent

I MISS THE LIFE THAT'S CALLING

one teaspoon, two teaspoons
of coffee into the boiling water, foam rising
and there's ringing in my ears, like a telephone
that never gets to voicemail.

one tablespoon and a half
of agave syrup, a touch of almond milk,
the coffee feels ready and there's an ape pounding
on my chest, a primal surge, a territorial claim
to protect my old story.

one sip, two sips
my morning is unfolding quite nicely
in perfect timing
in this cozy place
and now the phone is ringing with fresh news
and the kitchen is full of friends
and my lover is brewing coffee
and a tear rolls down one cheek
as the sun flashes across the other
and one foot shakes, restlessly
as if it stepped into another life
and my heart is growing limbs, pulling my ribs apart
as if escaping from jail,
i must be hallucinating this morning
it must be this coffee
it needs more sugar
to drown the bitter feeling
that today i won't be answering
the life that's calling

WHAT IS THE SOUL, I ASK

what is the soul, i ask
the undergrowth to highground,
the things you hear in the night of your fleshwound
in the stillness & the garbled sea,
sensing a world beyond yourself. there

soul is intact remembrance,
the flight poised at the edge of a valley,
a reasonless knowing of trajectory.

dark, potent, patient — like a seed or a crow feather
left in the depths of a forest
by forces unseen
riddled with the sounds of wild

soul demands a certain type of abandonment.
it demands that you leave things
but gives no comfort in the leaving.

the soul is what is asked of me, finally,
after all else collapses.

THE POSSIBILITY OF THINGS

when you are a poet
you live in the possibility of things
not the probability of things.
words like doorways
sifting through the landscape with our
heartheld lights
wondering at the wandering
careful not to stay too long
for an answer

when you are a poet, you are here not here
in a place between places
set on not settling
for a tea kettle whistling —
but instead following the sound
back through where it came from

i tell you, if you are a poet
you are a houseless thing
homebound and tongue-tied
at the profoundness of each moment,
as see-through as it is
glistening
into a million suns

I WANT MORE

i am, behind this, a vessel
that carries all things
and echoes the windlike secrets
into song.

behind this, i am roots into moreness
lessened by thoughts
patrolling the surface
attempting to break in.

but i rest behind windows, untouchable
in the unmovable silence
undeniable depths,
these are
my real friends
who want me to be more, not less.

i want more of what's behind this
not the rain, but where it comes from
and what it says that's so important
it's worth carrying water for.

i want friends like the rain —
pregnant
pressing
soulful nourishment.

behind me, my ancestors sit
at the mouth of the world, saying nothing
and i pretend i cannot hear them

in my bones, they are
patterns, passions — present

everywhere but in my moreness
for that is mine to focus forth

and carry
in this vessel, where the waters ring,
if you find me here, answering
i'll be curtainless, remembering
there's a real tune behind everything
it's a different kind of listening
and i vowed to feel it
spill it

sing.

PRESS ON

you, alone, must do this,
crawl your way towards the symbols
lead your feet into their ghostly doors
and wait for a voice of reason.

you, alone, must carry the thing
the only thing that's meant for you
that shifts the weight of the world
just because you carry it differently.

it's you, alone, in your ironswept clothes
that must brace the eternal fire
and be forged by a force greater than your own mind.

this force — ferrous and feral
prowling in the grasses, eyes lit,
will ask you to join the highlands,
become a hunter of new visions,
never prey to the old ways.

meet me at sundown in the dark woods,
come alone.

yes,
you, alone, must do this,
move snakelike unseen,
leave scent trails like a wandering ant
who's found the lip of something extraordinary.

the others will come.

then, you alone, must howl.
howl like the night depends on it,

like the valleys grow green by the slick pull of your tongue
like your guts sharpen their teeth to rip through the falsecries
and your wit digs its claws into the raw and the real,
feeding on the danger of
deep
dark
soulful living.

don't you be threatened by the shadows.
you are a shadow —
a shadow of no doubt
no hesitation,
a darkness you were born to carry and reveal
a striking contrast of quietude and screeching revival

and you are not alone in this.
many are watching.
many are being called to be the joints of truthflesh.
you are not alone
and still, you, alone, must do this.

MEANING

the morning is alive
wings lucid   endearing
weighed by some type of ready
i tossed and turned in the folds
like a century loaded with
change   waiting for directions
only doves can give

what matters
is the essence of the presence
the crisp yes
upon awakening   a gift
from the mouth of god
masking the noise
with better noise

plum, burgundy, amethyst
words that tossed and turned
in my mouth   before arriving
they don't want one meaning
they want many
like a salamander ready for land
but can't leave the water
it stays motionless   healing

you knew
what you came for
and the brave thing was not the coming
but the staying
in the stillness
where all the changes take place   unhindered
miscellaneous

i don't want one meaning
i want many

NIGHT PRAYER

let there be light
in the unending darkness
when the night is crawling
with the things unsaid

let there be light
in forgotten corners
in the under, deeper
where my sleep has fled

let there be light
and here be light
let there be wings
let there be flight
let there be love
let there be sight
let there be movement
without plight

and let the divine move you

first, you must know what you are, what paintings you're made of, what words turned to scars, what questions saved you, which threads are about to burst at the seams. and you must learn to love them. then you must enter your soulnight, swooning over the dark, allowing whatever must dissolve there to die gracefully. the dark is deciduous not to destroy but to prepare. whoever doesn't dare its depths cannot fully belong to the light. or even emerge into it. i believe we are here for the feeling of emerging — from the dark, from the prison of our minds, from ignorance, from the old ways into a new awakening world. many of your gifts&skills have a place in this emerging. then, as your patience simmers and your questions turn to "purpose", "belonging", even "destiny",

you must tune your ears to a voice that seems to come both from within and without.

you must recognize it, even endure it. you must know the difference between veil and veracity and follow the voice, not the echo. that's what it means to wait patiently before the dawn, to be called exactly as you are. not for what you might be, should be, could be. but this, today, you. if it calls you by your real name, then it'll take you to the places, people, and experiences you belong to. and that makes you fully free... because you won't have to be anything more or less than what you're made of and for. and that is ultimate freedom: the ability to share your authentic self. freedom is not about what you can get, it's about what you can give.

keep finding it in the little things. and follow the voice at every turn you make, trusting beyond sight. intuition speaks much like the deep dark does — without evidence, the way a lotus emerges, in subtle hums.

LIKE A CHILD IN A STREAM

it was brave what you did
back there
way way back
jumping into the waters like that
deaf to the shock.

welcome to the world, child
you had no way of knowing
that your ripples left the shore
left the jungles
left the earth
and reached a place beyond the knowing
of man.

continue playing
splashing, without rhyme or reason
because your chaos
is still
divine plan.

TRUST ME

and if you listen
deep down
a voice will say
"trust me"

what for and
where to?

if you soften
don't frail, just feel,
an inkling will creep through your bones
and stain them sweetly

why?
how?
what now?

i am made of questions, darling
answered by some voice
and the world speaks to me in a thousand languages
my life
arises in symbols
orchestrating some giant play
i know nothing about
giving directions
i can hear
but only some voice
can decipher.

YOUR SINGULARITY IS INFINITE

i am writing this for you, the one
that is watching
from the eyeful world.

there are days like these
when there is nothing to say
to do or be
and i feel imaginary.

still
words spill
and i am called to paper to tree
to ink to blood
and can call myself alive.

do you call yourself alive
when the world threatens to flatten you?
do you round into a planet
call on your own gravity
create your own universe
despite and inspite of everything?

do you replace one thought with another
one choice with a better
call it growth
keep going
fall back
give up, give in?
do you, like me,
see yourself in the advice you give another
and come home to gather your fragments
calling on the things you can't see?

i am writing this from a place you can't see
and you must've been calling on me
because i was calling on you, on us
to be closer, to be nearer, to be stronger
to build better, to BE better
darling
when helpless, restless, alone.

i am writing this, alone
with miles of lives behind me
and centuries of eyes ahead, looking back
from the orbit of all life —
we will be written in a book somewhere
one book, the only story, one author
the distance between alone and all-one;
no matter what character you play
can you accept it?

leave as is or change it?
come on now, you have the pen
you have the hand the heart the imagination
the drive the wisdom the ages and ages of breaths you took
in a million forms across the planets
in the spiral of life, wherever you coiled and uncoiled
yourself
you must've learned something, wanting something
as god for god through god
you left god and came back
erased language, brought it back
more alive than ever
use your mind your words
your will god's will, whatever
find that fire you are, alive, breathing
be the one you need the one you want,
the one you look up or through to

and power this universe.

if you're really all alone here, or all-one,
either way, your singularity is infinite.
if there's only you here
why'd you write this for yourself?

CENTER OF THE UNIVERSE

i look for center in all things
where life happens
why it moves out.

there is no sense
looking in branches for answers.
i have come for the core of life,
the seed,
the mystery behind mysteries.

i am tired of extremities —
the way they tangle
the way they fool.

i have come for god — from god,
and the distance between the two.
i'm here for the circling, to become
rounder
smoother
felt

sparkle & serenade.

to be darkness, buried, depth
risen & sought,

harvested.

slice this fruit down the middle
show me
how it began
to unleash a universe.

ELEPHANT SOUL

strong in its lead,
each step is a sureness.

there is no denying
the presence of the one that knows
that even a need of 600 pounds of food a day
is provided for.

to rise from your slumber
of unworthiness
is to find your elephant soul.
take up your space
trust life to find you.

WILLPOWER

in this moment of unpalpable will
mine or yours
i wonder how to
let go and
let god
when she
let go and
let me
come through
and have my own freedom

to choose to let
go or not
shine my being forth
or not
be the north star of higher consciousness
or not
god, have i done you wrong?

am i always between a yes or a no
right/wrong
pulled to extremes
by dual opposites?

perhaps my only choice
is to go willingly or not
for the going has been written
by a bigger hand

i am telling you, before this
you were a thought
in god's mind
and god was a thought

in yours
and we birthed one another
asking who's who.

when the light shines back, nodding
you will know your will is god's will.

save your willpower
for you will need it
when the mirrors multiply
and you don't know in which one you exist.

i am telling you, the power
of your will
dwells in planting it in good soil
and watering it daily.

let it grow rhythmically
to a solar pulse
and a lunar song,
surrender your will
to the free-verse poem that you are
and god will power
you.

A STONE HEART

have a stone heart
one that knows what it wants
openings in the ridge

have a stone heart
place-filled and eloquent
weathering the storm

have a stone heart
whispers from the domed soul
giving off a scent

of a stone heart
bold, assuming nothing
ready when the time comes

it's my stone heart
carrying light heavy-handed
ready to pour

ask your stone heart
where to sit
and be ancient
patient
ready

GOD IS HOMELESS

knocked at the temple, god wasn't there
not in the nun's eyes, absent and bare
behind the altar, silver and gold
an offer to god but god isn't sold

i left for the mountains, rivers of light
nature gave me a direct line of sight
of the countless forms in which god can partake
the leaf and the boulder, the bee and the lake.

yet i still haven't found him in his true flesh and bone
i'm starting to think that god isn't home
i even turned inward to seek god inside
but something or someone must've left him untied

no trace of god in the rooms of my heart
just his belongings, poems, and art
visions and dreams, color and song
places god visits but doesn't stay long

so where is god lately, where does he reside
by what means do i purchase a ticket to ride?
a man comes to me and says with a smile
i can take you to him but let's walk for a while

so he utters a poem with his liquor-stained breath
walks the streets shoeless, hiding from death
frayed at the edges and slightly insane
homeless and dirty, a man with no name

and i start to feel a bridge coming through
connecting two islands out of the blue
the man that is me, the me that is you

the oneness of god is undoubtedly true

he knows there are many looking for him
on the road to repentance, in service and sin
but god takes up residence in the last place you'll go
he is the nothing and nowhere you fear to know

when you find him, it's simple, he was there all along
an awareness just seeking your eyes to belong
you'll be caught in a paradox, nowhere to go
'cause my dear, god is homeless, when you see it, you'll know.

CHOOSE YOUR MADNESS

do not lose your head in this madness,
it's not your kind.

to your own madness stay true, wrapped
in your soul vines. yes,

even your soul deals in vines and veils
tricks to keep you on the path.
but its roots are loveborn.

you have been digging the earth, looking
for truth in complexity,
dealing in fragments.

take your head out of the dirt,
roots all look the same.

relax, sit back, and watch as it all
simply breaks the surface,
then you will know weed from wildflower.

at last,
go madly innocent
fall into the bloom.

GOD'S WISH

i couldn't ask for more
than what is here right now
because i'm everything
creation's silent vow

a petal in a dream
a rose, a master-piece
and the master inside me
wants nothing more than this

i want and have it all
and nothing's without me
yet in this sky arose
a timely kind of dream

for spring to come again
for all to rise anew
as if it came for me
as if i pulled it through

but what joy would that be
if spring came when i called
so i made it once-removed
and then its coming stalled

slowly, the winter passed
and spring was a surprise
but i already knew
how spring looks through my eyes

so i gifted all of me
to love's eternal reach
and let it spread its seedlings

and gave it space to teach

love became everything
a wild creative source
and awed by her pure essence
i split my single source

who else to bring love home
like springtime roses do
oh human, can't you see it?
that's when i wanted you.

LOVEFILL

just a ray of sunshine in the morning
unfiltered
a rise is coming, pink and tender
dew-aged, we are returning
to the seat of the window inside us, to the stars that made us
but have not defined us,
left us wandering
the cosmic gap
that became our lovefill

we were made for this
type of filling — sweet, fiery, a rush
a type of wild marrow
that lets you run loose in the mornings.

if you taught your shadow
how to dance
then let it teach you how to fall, dark&empty
so you rise lovefilled,
like a cup of sun

IT IS WRITTEN

i want to reach you
arms over water
speak in one language
with my hundred tongues

i want to enter
secret doors
drop keys in wells
only for the thirsty

there are facades to break
and we only have these hands
so there must be faith
that is stronger than flesh
faith that exceeds
faith that opens
faith that leads
faith that hopens

we need invisible hands
to tear down
invisible barriers

i know their language
hands, barriers
givers, carriers
waiting for us

to find each other

in the signs
all ancient and gleaming
hanging from doorways

unspoken

get closer

what is written
is wanting
to reach us

through the wound

you see, i have an eye for where the light comes through. backlit leaves. reflective glass. sunrays through a tree opening. late afternoon slithers of light. i don't look for it, it looks for me. do you have something that always looks for you like this?

rumi says, "the wound is where the light enters you". but i also believe,

the wound is where the light leaves you and reaches others, like a bird flying out through an open window.

once the wound is invited to be part of your wholeness, it is an orientation through which you can be of service to the world. like the ancient japanese art of kintsugi, you fill up your cracks with gold — and that's what makes you beautiful&rare.

perhaps we are so attuned to the light because we have spent time in the darkness. perhaps our only fight is to become more&more transparent, to let go of what makes us opaque&resistant, and to let the light through.

we must crack open wider. speak to each other from the depths, not from the safety of our shallows. share unpracticed feelings. yes? maybe then we would belong to place&people a little more organically.

the sun consciousness represents our higher self. sometimes it casts shadows so you can seek the source of the light. sometimes it shines directly so you can be always home, always home, always home. and other times, when nearest to the horizon, when closest to the night, it says: darling, be a clear thing and let me work through your windows.

CARCASS

we feed on old things, in new ways
that is the spiral of life
and whoever calls it a circle
simply doesn't know
why things must die.

any carcass will tell you
the secret of life:

that you will live it — the secret, that is —
devour it
as a mystery,
as a question
never coming back on itself
though it pretends to

and when you get to the end
of your own tail
that is a beginning
of a different tale —
this is how
you live in all the books you've ever read
and ever will;
there, infinite and proud.

knowing thyself is one thing
that takes many lifetimes,
living thyself is another
and that takes now.

to be infinite is not to eventually come back
to some starting point,
but to be here

and to keep going.

your time is merely a carcass you beflesh
you are all of it
and all that passes on
passes through,
becomes part and
moves into you
and that's how you feel the ribs of a carcass
pressing into your own
as death presses into life
to help it come alive.

for it is life that calls forth death
it is soul that calls forth flesh
it is mind that calls forth matter —
in any extreme, you will find the other,
and in the center you are turning
like the key that you are.

have you seen your beauty lately
what makes you human, alive
what rattles your bones in flight
and brings you here, doorwide?

even as all things return to oneness
yes, even you,
it is not the same oneness
as the one that decided to split
into many doors —
just as the you that loses your keys
is certainly not the same you
that finally finds them.

THIS, HERE

here, & it's okay
if not there, if not that
but this, here, all there is
and all that should be.

i've waited centuries for this, here
i have been that, there a thousand times.
it's time for this, here, now.

don't leave who you are for what you should be.
don't leave.
stay here. stay now. milk the ground.

this, here will take you everywhere you're meant to.
leave a footprint.
day in and day out, you must continually leave that, there
and move in a way different
than what you had planned.
beyond want & need,
own this, here. and sink your feet in enough
to keep walking.

BONES

when you go back into the womb of the earth, it remembers
your name
your real name, and the words
come alive from every page you ever wore
like coats in the dead of winter, alive you
sang yourself to yourself
and the whole world heard those ghosts you sent
in the dead of winter, towards spring
ghosts &visions, i know them,
i've met them — where i met myself
we have danced with these bones,
piles and piles of bones, in the dead of winter
ancestors that held our ankles
and we held their visions in our flesh, hot
hesitating at the step forward
to rise higher, on these piles of bones
in the dead of winter, you will hear them
from every corner of your life — whispering
where they have been, where we must go
with all this love in the bones
bones that break
bones that heal
bones that rise
bones that know and have always known
your other names
rise from the dead, darling
with your other names, rise
i know what it looks like on the outside
but oh, these insides
are wildly alive

SURFACE LIGHT

it's all you need
after you traveled the depths
or were born from them,
surface light
to have a little
to get by

there in the womb
of extreme darkness
the monsters naturally
summon your light

but here
here at the surface stream
where things seem but aren't
where faces pass like questions
and winter drags its feet, scraping
the flesh that keeps you in,
all this fog
will fool you

old friends from distant places
keep your going,
all else, trick&mirror
creates drag

and you,
you beautiful ancient songrise
you stunningly soaring creature
must do the smallest thing
with nimble fingers
and press on your surface light:

shine it only on this moment,
this thing
whatever you are doing now
is sacred work

& you are the one
that needs your kindness
you are the one
that needs your preaching
you are the one
that needs the watering, the tending, the careful hand
the final decision to be in joy
while waiting for it
to live the thing you're truly made of
and light the world in ways only you can,
we can't
without you
we need your deepwaters

and for that
you must brave the surface winds
for that
you must be in the world but not of it
for that
you must rise elegantly above the allness
that seems to be but isn't

for that, my love
press on, press on

DESIRES

every day, you must know what you are wanting
because therein lies your weakness
and your wings.

in the desire of belonging
lies the trappings of a cult,
stealing your mind and your senses.

in the desire of being wanted
waits a mate
that will make of you whatever he wishes
and certainly not what you wanted to become.

in the desire of riches
your heart leaves home.

do not desire anything outside yourself
because you will have it
and it will only lead you back
to yourself.

don't leave at all
desire to become, not to have
for the having follows being
and your being is no place for a trap.

THERE IS NO SPOON

morning in a time like this says
slow down, return, remember
drink your coffee, let it settle
put your spoon down slowly because it, too,
creates ripples
everything creates ripples
there are tidal waves out there
and i can't help anyone if i am drowning.

mourning in the morning
takes so many forms
speaking from all corners
in all kinds of tongues
shouting over one another
and i must hear myself
spoon out the absolute.

i think of recent friends
the way we all keep each other afloat
and others
you, perhaps,
living like a mystery inside my heart
and all that makes me who i am
and who i need to be

this morning and all mournings
open me up for a reason, a season, a lifetime
like friends do
like lovers, wildflowers, and daydreams
so i can remember
that there is no spoon
except the one i'm holding right here and now.

WHAT YOU SEEK

little by little, we move towards what we want,
we have to,
regardless of what tries to push without.

little by little, we swell with creation
until we become a planet
moved by its own gravity.

every single movement changes the cosmic pattern,
even a single sip.

i want a center of love,
galactic arms of meandering hope
reaching the unknown.
i want a life full of life —
to be the cup,
become filled,
to be the liquid flowing over the edge,
become wooden tray
inch towards the tea kettle,
crawl home.

i want to be put back on the stove
turned on by a hand that knows me,
burn alive,
leave the waters
become steam
and rain down hard,
quench everything,
drown the silence
storm away
and come back wanting more.
i want to remain cloud-turned, a whirling soul

sufi-centered
ancient-rooted
human-bound
turn earthlike, windsputtered, windsung
blow in chaos
and out of it
make perfection.

i want to lay down to rest, finally,
in a body somewhere, fall asleep for centuries,
like a tired god
forgetting where i've been
who i've been
what i've wanted.

i'm tired, god.

and perhaps one day i'll turn into the morning,
a spontaneous decision
to spontaneously combust
into a sunrise-spilling paintcan
and i'll open my eyes in a warm bed,
get up,
boil water,
make tea,
and write this poem.

SUMMON YOUR WHOLENESS

monsters out of this closet
i'm battling things
both mine&not mine
it doesn't matter what it is
but what i become at the end of this

bring them all home
make them tea
open wide enough for anything
to come in and die inside you

you must be a place for death
love, life, resurrection
but first invite everything
to become something more.

you are more than any monster
you have shelter
storm
and thunder

summon your love
like you summon your demons
all at the same time
let them meet
become whole together.
love was made for demons
like light was made for dark
all were made out of each other, for each other
and you are the place in which they meet
the one thing between two things
seeming like a third thing,
becoming whole.

HOLY SPACES

what is wholeness
but seeing that i am made of holes
bullet-ridden
and only like this my flesh is called
to close in on the healing

the quest for a light source starts
with casting a shadow on the pavement

what is wholeness
but finding rest in restlessness
and belonging in the longing
traversing distances empty dark wide bridges unknown leaps
wholeness darling
is making all your spaces
holy

SWEET MENDING

this year's harvest of honey is dark&deep
much like the center of the soul
and all that magik
goes unmute

gather the stars
for you will swallow them
when your pieces crumble

kintsugi
nurture your nature
fill up

we are arriving at the place we came from
like some type of reverse osmosis

all night
i'm consciously asleep
so you can wake
from a bad dream — pull the trigger
every aim, every demon
every apple, every garden
belongs to one seed
so
go
deep, dark
live dangerously outspoken
on the prowl
trickling
gold between the pieces

beyond the edge

FINDING THE WITNESS: A MEDITATION

i found my voice
and another and another
spiraling to the edges of myself
this edge and the next
and each voice claims to be the last

i found my voice but it is not my voice
an impostor, certified
vowing to translate my wholeness
and missing the mark

this is the last voice and this must be it
my true voice that reigns over all voices
that one that knows them all

but this too, is not my voice

i have lost my voices and called no more to them
in silence
i am awareness itself

then a voice found me and said
"you are this voice but not this voice"
and that seemed wise
so then i spoke
from all voices yet none
"i am the voice
that loses many
and lastly
finds itself"
but that too, was not it

there is but one voice

it sings but one song
i am but one verse
and this too, is not it

BEACON

hello, is anybody out there
and will any body answer
this beacon clawing at the world
bottomless

i have nothing to give
and it took me a long time
to get it

over this abyss, i am
indigo waters of spilled ink
an island, adrift

lost, found wandering
lost, aiming at nothing
but land, to land, somewhere
some foreign territory
you

MEET

it is how we get closer
to whatever sings &shines &sees
to each other, in these turbulent times of need and needed
as the intimate becomes the ultimate.

it is how we, slowly, inch
towards one and the same mad breath
and lose our fittings. we need each other
washed clean, stripped by the oncoming rapids.
i have been looking for a way
to release the need of chasing the stream,
and let it instead flow into me
taking what it must.

i am somewhere loud, anchored in the silence
a tiny precious eye
will you meet me there
meet me there
and kiss
whatever's left.

CUTTING THE PEACH TREE

one branch of one tree, cut
felt like one branch of all trees
felt like all arms across all worlds
no longer reaching

i was thirteen
i was thirteen thousand
in a garden with a peach tree being cut down

and it said to me:

when the world cuts wider you also
become wiser, darling,
when you
hurt deeper you can
heal louder, darling,
when life
feels heavier you can
rise freer, darling

enlightenment is simply knowing
there is nothing lost

DEAR FEAR, MY FRIEND

where does fear grip you
but in your chest
in that silent sponge
that takes no rest

and it wants me pinned
to my early grave
it will crepp right in
and become a wave

but if i stretch my arms
and become the sea
i will grow beyond
all the fear in me

and i call these waves
and the ships they bring
they will gather love
they will laugh and sing

and the song will say
love is what i am
and those who come to me
will become my friend

dear fear, my friend
you have rights to be
but you're a tiny wave
and i'm the whole damn sea.

WISHLESS

moved by the silence, i whimper to a stop
and plunge into ceremony
of stillness.

i have come with nothing
i expect the same.

i want to be full of zeroes
fresh starts
untouched land.

but, that too, is a wish.

this forest fills
and i can't name what.

i let go of names
the word "squirrel"
let go of forest
hike
me
stillness
let go completely

wishless

WINDFUL

wind carries with it
news,
things that i must know
and only those.

i listen by ridding myself of doing
and thinking about doing.

orange poppies grow not knowing
the secrets they spill
of how water flows to every leaf
and the world takes care of itself
with or without me
with or without me
the world sings in doorways
and you wake every morning
with the keys in your flesh
a desperate quest of unlocking
everything you touch
across the spheres
i'll have the wind bring
the drums of my bones
and carry them on
with or without me
i'll have you know
that i have been touched by everything
touched everything
windful or not.

6 FEET APART

in a world 6 feet apart & masked
i want to be closer, maskless
worse, open, spilling
melting into each other

in a world 6 feet apart & masked
your eyes are all i have and all i need
and finally i am looking

across the distance, reaching
with a thousand arms
the ones you can't see
the ones that make me, me
caught in the vastness of the space between us
each time i fall

and fall i do
for the love of falling
for the love of flying
and discovering new worlds

yours, i hope
in the vastness of crowds
reaching from one place to another
with their thousand arms
nearer and nearer to being reached

we are, the reached
enriched
when no distances matter
and no matter distances us
from the soul within

6 feet apart & masked
but you know a smile when you feel one
there in the spirit between us, spilling freely
infecting the space

you think i'm 6 feet apart & masked
but i'm running wild
in and out of people
dancing with their souls

MEDICINE FROM THE DEEP DARK CAVES

all this singing
is meant to be done in a deep dark cave
the dancing, in a deep dark cave
the dreaming, the loving, the praying
away from the eyes of the world
into the soul of the world
touching the dreams of the world
bare-handed dreamers, we
with our shattering rhythms
we with our deafening spirits
administering the cure directly

art of smoke & mirrors
creeping into the veins
fur clad, slipping under the canopy soundless
shadowswept
with the power of the wound

this is the healing

invincible
and traceless
downright scarred but nameless

we, the seedcarriers
the firetenders
the soulsingers
the woundwakers
find us in the deep dark caves
where you have feared to go, we live there
in the deep dark caves

witches and wizards

magical creatures, endangered
drinking moonlight by the fireside
tangled in a weave of lights, laughing
and bottling the laughter
as medicine

yes, someone needs to be
in the deep dark caves
echoing the light

E KOMO MAI

be still ... and
let the stillness speak

"   "

what moves around you is both you&notyou
and you must know which is when

winds come trading secrets with the rain, mmm
if you are listening.. quiet, quieter now
letting the world in {

all doors are open today
flexible on their hinges
made of palm fronds and sweet fruit peels
inviting the bliss

you must make a home for bliss
yes, out of your origin of stillness
a sanctuary of color
of crystal and god ~
carpets of kindness
and sweet sweet songs, whatever they feel
as long as they are real

bliss enters gently, unsuspecting
like rain clouds & rainbows
a butterfly crossing your peripheral vision
e komo mai

the stillness comes alive in you
and this, darling,
is the only way to move

everything dissolves
especially the hinges
and then
there is no other noise
not even
this poem

HE>I

god lures you to the edge
throws you overboard
into your life

and you must cease grasping the waves
become ocean
become the way

& into the love you belong to

how do i speak of love without saying the word "love"?
i weave it into birdsong out of my verseless heart that wants
what it already has. to want what you have is to know the
sacred piece of belonging.

and that is love without saying it is love, for when you name
it, it half-disappears.

*love only comes when you're done calling for it and you simply become
what lives up to its name.*

there is no perfect place to find love, no perfect thing to love.
start here, this is good practice. start with you, your hand,
this plant, your hand on this plant, the green that enters you,
this foreign thing, "the other", making its way through the
ten thousand names you carry, weaving a new story.

this is how you let love in, "the other", open to the invasion
of a nameless force.

{   }

it is a wild bird
listen
you cannot touch it
listen
and move slowly
filling your birdfeeder
with seeds
knowing that love
shall come to feed.

THE EDGELESS YOU

the soul wants to be seen at daybreak, roaring
and sifting through candlelight shadows
seen in its aching
leaping, scraping against the rough times, seen
beautiful in its rising

the soul needs real friends and real lovers
the ones that feel like sweetwater
the ones under one name, the True Friend,
that see you in your truth and flame
call you by your real name.
woman, go find them.

by scent and sound you'll know them
see through the veils
share space with them
share ritual and twilight
soul song and foresight
come closer to the edgeless you.

TRUE FRIENDS

we have true friends from other places
places we have known but left
places we have been but changed
places we return to in our sleep.
we have true friends, invisible
leading part of the way
bringing questions to our answers
like all true friends do.
they live in stars, supernovas
in bodies and out of them
in timelines and between them —
we know their stillness.

they sleep in books
and play in the fields with us
aligning signs from the other side.
these are friends
we take cue from
for they are polished mirrors
like all true friends are.
the most alive i've ever seen, friends
who transcend timelines, souls
alive everywhere.
that's the only way i want to live —
in one life, continuing
with my one red thread
tied to the absolute.
meet me there
in placeless ways
and be my friend.

OCEAN OF YOU

breath aligned
we become each other
you, me
and i, you
forming an art
of cosmic light unfinished

our skins, like barriers
that keep us from the oneness
just to lead us back into it

i stumble at the plunge
drowning
sinking
so deep in
that i emerge
on the other side
and start dreaming
with your heart

A SONG I KNOW

i find home in strange places
at the feet of butterflies
under string lights in a garden at night
in the eyes of someone
i met only yesterday
you

home in the slow down, breathe, there is only now
only us
on the rim of a cup
too full and ready to spill

into the abyss i came from
the one i'm returning to
the one i know you from

i wrap myself in
a song i know
your voice
a verse i have yet to understand

LIGHTWEAVER

at twilight, i seek the light
scooped up from the undergrowth by birdsongs.
i hear love coming.

i wake with the sun, i become the sun
the center of my life.
all things are a different verse from my heartsong.

i do not feel like one thing.
i toss in my bed of flowers, eager to decide.
morning comes and i am undecided.
i have opened all the doors and windows.
i have become them. i have become everything
instead of one thing.
now... how to start the day?
who starts the day?

the two-light, of course.
the in-between dreamsleep and lovesong,
the breath before word that is the word.
the sillhouette of want,
reaching its hand out towards the lushness.
the humble gratitude of
this, now, here, the only thing.

whatever you want, you are that already.
listen. love is here.
and it doesn't sound nor look like one thing.

i know how i'll start the day.
i'll be whatever love needs me to be.

CILANTRO

over cilantro, i came up to you
finally, with a reason
to say something
reasonable
"hi, do you have any more cilantro in the back of the store?"
but what i really meant to say was
you, with that golden gaze, captivate me
each time i come here
"we do, in fact, we just received a shipment not long ago"
i receive you
through my skin
ears mouth ribcage collarbone

your secret thoughts run down my skin
like springtime rivers —
"oh perfect"
we are in a meadow, taking the world in
speaking in flowers
laughing in color
soiled to the bone
eyes wrinkled in joy
"we should restock it in the next 5 minutes"
we must be 5 doors too early or 5 doors too late, i don't know
why things align the way they do
and people too
"great, i will wait"
forever
is undressing itself, eternal layers
unveiled in stolen corners
of weekday shopping
or starry midnights
as we are rolling down grassy hillsides
stripped sentiments

are spilling into the soil around us
turning to seeds
and one day we will look back
to see what grew

oh look,
cilantro

WHAT IF

you, that touch
do i begin
where it ends
it's a question
of wholeness
of what if
i lead
my life
like this
what if
it's good
it's best
it's better
it's all that you ever wanted
what if
i dissolved completely
piece by piece
past present future
what if now
i am this thing
i can't explain
us
i am
a what if
in a cocoon
of possibility
of infinite yes
of a wingspan as wide
as my lovespan
what if i don't end
where you begin
and this touch
is a messenger

of the spark
where stars create themselves
and we are somewhere at center
in the pulse
in the shadows
in the light
in the beginning and ending of time
what if
i am a butterfly
in god's chest
and there are a million in mine
fluttering wild
spilling from my mouth
into yours
crossing dimensions
they didn't know they could
becoming infinite
infinite and free
like you
like me
what if

THE MOTH THAT SURVIVES

without you, i couldn't have done it
without the yes in my heart
without the doors off their hinges, laughing
and you taking me in, again and again
dissolving into the shine

how can i be tamed
without you, impossible
without you the perish is probable
but i am the moth that survives
i am the flame that thrives, fire
that cleanses, water that spills at the feet
of your life, it's you and it's me
it's the we that survives
this initiation
ceremonial burn, burn wild
burn alive, come clean, come true
you
without
i wither in the
fields, a flower with no name
in the field of the evening
i call voiceless and you wait
behind the answer
smiling

HOW COULD YOU NOT

how could you not
fall in love, fall in love, fall
in love
with all the things that come to you and through you
with all the madness and genius
the signs of the times
the sign that it's time
to let more through
how could you not
fall apart
at the sight of the sky
mouth open eyes wide
break into pieces
gather back, gather
wander into the night, wander
know what is not you
and see much better
at first sight
all the signs are curious
curious and clear
fall into them
fall & follow
time stopped and you began, alive
a supernova sky
wingspoken
lovesighted
freefalling

A LINK UNKNOWN

i'm literally crumbling, he says
detangling the pieces, slow take
in the fast lane
watching the world spin by
and i
have no say in this heart, the way
it beats towards what makes it
come alive, you
us
a link unknown, made up by
some magical creature, universal spin
a laugh across the ages, echoing
i hear my life in pieces
too many doors to count
lives lived, unlived, relieved
and i want to sit by a door
breathing, with you
a storm around us forming the pieces
feeling vivid
colorful, like some magical creature
from a distant dream
i left only yesterday

ALOHA KE AKUA

love speaks in many languages
it'll take me a lifetime to learn them all —

it speaks in sense & scents
and simplicity
it says yes and it says no
it's still, it's sparkling
slithering
it slays and soothes
speaks through everything
when you are everything

where you will rise

AMOR INFINITO

así, conozco una flor que tiene alas. que tiene colores como el
crepúsculo, que se extiende siempre al revez del cielo. no
importa a dónde o con quién o cómo; para ella, solo importa
que vuela, así, utilizando sus raizes como huesos que
sostienen su vuelo. no sé cual tipo de flor es, de donde viene,
y por donde se va. sé solo que parece una flor y se mueve
como una mariposa. sin razón o lógica, así, atraída por la
dulzura de la vida. pero tiene lindos colores, y los conosco
bien. y son, al mismo tiempo, colores de la tierra y del cielo,
siempre intercambiandose. pero cómo sostener una flor que
vuela? cómo darle agua o viento? cual necesita y cuando? yo
nunca sé. pero este es mi corazón. necesita muchas cosas. y
yo sé solo esto, que las mariposas hacen largos viajes y las
flores se abren al sol. entonces, si ella es tanto una mariposa y
una flor, yo tengo que ser algo más grande, como el cielo,
como un camino de libertad por su ascenso, un envase para
la luz. sí, esto es lo que soy para mi corazón — un espacio
grande que contiene todo: luz, agua, viento. en fin, amor
infinito.

A SECRET IN WAITING

open yourself enough
to receive the magic
your heart is built for.
walk the amethyst ways,
become the crystal that you are.
there is no doing in the reaching
there only this moment, in being, realized.
i sit to translate the one song.
i sit so deeply that i become it.
there is no more translation.

this is a tiny thread of wovenhood,
a monumental leap in matter.
what matters is that your heart is still here,
telling you secrets.
widen your openings.
you are a bigger secret in waiting.
follow the winged creatures' way.
chase nothing but freedom.
you will catch it mid-flight.
there is nothing to do or say this morning,
there is only the flutter in my ribcage
walls cracking
wings
dancing
free.

STRAIGHT HOME

this is the opening, the only type of opening
that makes your heart peel —
feeling golden,
a conductor for all good things,
a shape of hope.

i feel
wingspoken.

it is like this, when you're airborne, windful,
something else is beating your wings,
something bigger than all you have carried
bigger than skill
than preparation
it is love itself, needing no names
no memory
no home,
for it is one.

larger than heart
than vow
than anticipation
let it speak for itself

in the opening
when you find that you are giving in
walking blindly towards what you have resisted
and straight home.

BIRTHING THE NEW

i have been carrying centuries in my womb,
left carrying alone,
left.

i have fled through doors and doors, leaving the harbor
moon after moon, running from the spilled blood.
walls are bleeding with the echoes of an ache so powerful,
it has left me raw.
i, woman, carrier, nurturer,
wisdom keeper of the ancient stories,
awaken in the midst of crimson.
these are my tears and not my tears,
the crying of womanhood.

what is releasing is also healing, the ages of victimhood,
the stains of what has been taken by force.
i have preferred to be rootless,
for without roots no one can reach the depths of me,
for without roots, there is the safety of turning away
from the darkness.
for without roots,
there is no worry of what to take in.
without roots, we are less porous.
without roots, we can choose flight at any time.
without roots, there is no impending danger of whatever
lurks in the dark earth.

but without roots, i am drying. without roots, the womb feels
the weight of every abandoned place on earth.
and it is crying out for love and gentleness and the sweet slow
extending into the warm and living earth.
i am this living earth.
there are words in this womb.

there are all the lives i've touched and all yet to be touched,
nurtured by the crimson floods of a rhythm
i have yet to understand.
the divine speaks and dances, moves me through laughter
and tears at a pulsing pace.

shedding, i am creating a new story.
shedding, i am revealing what has not worked.
shedding, these are the shadows without voice,
the child with too many nightmares to count.
shedding, i am still here.
shedding, there is life through and though and i,
for a moment, carry the womb of creation.
infinity rests here, in the roots of me
falls asleep in my arms, wakes up to the morning warmth.

i am letting go and letting through.
this is one too many wounds to carry,
the final ache before the healing,
the bursting sprout before the rooting.

i carry infinite grace. i carry forward momentum.
i carry every dream into creation.
in this womb, there is aching.
if there is aching, there is healing.

as women, we have birthed gentleness, and kindness,
and nourishment. we have birthed fields and fields of
wildflowers, taught the world how to turn towards the light.
it is time we claim ours.

it is time we birth the new earth into being.
it is time to let out what has been kept hidden.
let it send its roots deep and far, find its own nourishment.
there is so much love to be had, to be made, to become.

with love, i am allowing the body its process.
with love, i nourish myself as much as i nourish the world.
with love, i dissolve into infinity, a soul among many,
an energy honored to be part of the one.

i am a woman, one among many, carrying the eternal womb,
releasing the damage, embracing the flow.
i honor this moment, this body,
as it slips slowly under the moonlight into the dark earth for
nourishment — precious and softening.

tomorrow, we rise again, full as the moon,
claiming and reclaiming our growth.
this is rebirth.
this is our journey.
over and over again, heavy and shedding,
aching and healing,
curling in the womb of the earth
to awaken again and again.

LET THE WATERS THROUGH

but darling have you seen the way
the edges curl sometimes,
holding the first rain
dreading the drought —
that is us, living the dream
and,
fearing it gone,
attempting to seal it.

loosen your grip. you
are a cactus no longer.
release
your holding
let the waters return.

sweetness is here.
what will you do with it today?
there are a thousand ways to bitterness
and only one to truth,

the one that stirs your mountains
enough that the echoes don't return
the one that tickles
the only one that knows and waits and opens for every drop
of you
and changes with the sun
and withers by the moon and dies to itself
the resurrection as witness
responding with love
for that is your highest power.

let every mirror be clear.

so much movement in this stillness
in distillness, pure spirit
innocent as rain
is filling the green i am becoming
the green i am protecting
green is
the way i breathe
the way i feed
the way i heal.

the first color there ever was
green,
full of sun and rain
bursting open into flower
spilling into fruit —
that is us
and our gifts
when we let the light move
and the waters through.

EVERY HONEST THING WAS MADE TO SPILL

things look a little different today
the neighbor's house sitting on its grassy lawn
like a lego toy
the yard filled with chickens while the cat looks on
curious
trees
filling their lungs with air — motionless
some picture from a distant dream — childless
and i am spinning around it, inside it
caught in the reel.

i feel real today
the sun cracked through my window at dawn
and went right through me
like i was made of glass
like i was made of no thing —
every thing
opens eventually.

every honest thing
was made to spill

and i spill in fragments
over secret lips
over cliff edges and sea shores
colors, dreams, and all

are there cups to catch me,
transparent and glassy?
what am i made of? wordless things.
and for?
a play thing in a player's world,
wandering edgeless

filled to the brim with hope
waiting to spill on a day like this.

cloudless and quiet,
but i swear it poured last night
there was a sea everywhere
and i was every thing,
spilled from every edge
and somehow today
everything is filling.

TODAY I FEEL LIKE

today i feel like
some kind of bird
windruffled and airbone
straight into the longlasting bliss

today i move like
a crow at the edge of the darkness
turning its head to the mountain at dawn.

today i sing like
a sage-scented window
giving thanks to the frame that defined me.

today i burn like
the phoenix, the mountain, the sage
cleansing and crowing
rising and growing
past the tip of the morning —
alive.

to live lively
is a gift you give to yourself.
unwrap, my friend
come free of the doing
let the being take form.

30 YEARS

it only took 30 years
to have a nutella croissant for breakfast
and not worry about 1001 things
the ways i could've eaten better
some healthy person i'm missing out on
if i don't have carrot juice
it only took 30 years to spend money on this
and that
not this or that
30 years
to say yes when i want to say yes
to say no when i want to say no
simple but
30 years
to feel the moment for the moment
for me, not for my camera reel or instagram
for my 355 distant friends
or some faceless followers
who are missing their own moment
to look at mine
30 years
to put the word "nutella" in a poem
because i thought nutella doesn't belong in a poem
but all of me belongs in a poem
and it, too, can be timeless
took me 30 years
to be timeless
love every laugh line and not try to fix it
always fixing, healing, dragging
for 30 years
i had no idea that fixing who i am
gives me no time to love
me or anyone else

that perfection is what we are
and our power and beauty is infinitely magical
fantastical
and we are raised afraid of it
30 years
and that was my biggest fear
not spiders not snakes not sharks
not even death
only the magic i hold.
30 years to create a small story
and finally graduate
and for this they give no diplomas
30 years to learn how to ask for help
30 years to sing with the bedroom window open
because the neighbors might hear
to cry in public
to go climbing and learn how to fall
to tell every soul what i love about them
and not hold back
to conquer the limits that aren't even mine
30 years to know what's mine and not mine
and not get caught up in the mix
30 years, i mean that's a wrinkle in time
a laugh line
a hairpin in the universal tresses
a sliver of god
god who loves the inner journey
god who loves dancing
god who loves ghandi
god who loves khalid
god who loves old churches
god who loves fresh nightclubs
god who loves canyons, meadows, oceans
abandoned buildings
rooftop bars

trains
bare feet
solitary mornings
gathered evenings
and everything in between
a mix of extremes and curiosities
30 years to learn how to keep up with myself
and love every piece
feel guilty for none
30 years to feel like she's perfect
30 years to worship her
not some idea, not some standard of who i want her to be
30 years and she's sparkling
30 years and i'm in awe every day of life in every way
30 years to love life
MY life
and not want to be anywhere else as someone else
30
to feel like my life has arrived
although i know it's been knocking all along
and maybe 30 more
to realize it's always arriving, continually knocking
yes come in
yes yes yes
i'm here for you, i'm all in for you
we're home, we're safe
and life is absolutely shining, crystalline
sexy
sparkling
soothing
silly
spectacular
claim it
it's yours
now

not in 30 years, not next moment
not "when i..."
but now right here, all you are
this whole
THIS
is the gift
unwrap, celebrate, sink deep
30 years deep

LET US GO REASONLESS

to be bodywise in a world of mind
of must
and muster up
is to pause and tune your ear
to an infinite mouth
and feel guiltless
lined up with a force of a river
no human mustering can summon

when the body says 'no'
rest here
rest her
say yes to a 'no' without reason
because reason might be the end of us

i say let us go reasonless
run through the meadow for the meadow
for you
for the sun to shine
in you
in all things wise in their bodies — of water
reasonless for joy

if you want to be happy
let something else have the right of way
something more elegant than mind
and much more intelligent

IN THIS FIELD

let us all go home together
not asking what that means,
and move into the light speechless
our mouths spilling
with wildflowers.

this is a scent we'll always remember
deep into the cosmic dream.

friends, lovers
i no longer know the lines between us,
we are all lovers here.

this whole journey
is a love affair
with the mystery within each other.

we meet in this field, finally
meaningless yet moving
like wind.

WE ARE ALL SECRET LOVERS

learning love in all kinds of languages
we meet in all kinds of fields
have been in all types of houses
we are all in love with each other, i know it

bound by spirit
by blood
by coffee
it doesn't matter, what spills
is necessary
it must spill
it must be free
to entere and leave us
wound and heal us

within and between
all of us, strangers
we are all secret lovers
bound by everything
connected
re-source full

until the silence speaks
until there is no freedom
as loud as us or what we are
when we become it
love
freedom
spirit
let these words dissolve here
be born in some other way
in some new field, wandering
in a body

yours

finally free

...

seeds drop
and a sound emerges
the birth of the world is the birth of the world

you
with eyes
untethered
come closer

to speak with this many mouths
creates many ears
all funneling into one

distilled spirits
leaving and entering bodies
leaving and entering mouths leaving and entering
it is happening beyond the shell
into the chaos we were born into
the order we return to

become unclasped

like a seed in the soil damp with yes
cracking and crying
seething and sighing
drinking the sky down
waiting on waiting
you're suddenly
free

YOU BECOME FREE BY FREEING

what does it mean to be free
i'm looking at you
words on paper   wanting release from
all the lines   the pretty ways
we set ground   to look elsewhere
one the next page   freedom waves
and i wave back, shy   wanting to know
what becomes of the story (yours, mine)
if words lift off a page
golden and   destined to be
perched at the edge of a landscape unknown
like a god so full she might spill
into a kind of stupor
that creates worlds
someone will read this   in their lonely nights
and we'll carry the lonely together
because there's ever only one of us here
and that makes us holy
holy & free

and i curl at the edges like a page wanting to   run

and speak of nothing but the sun
a universal language   symbols of the light shadow
wisdom

when we go uncaged, a little blind
unbridled
across a room, across fields
of paper   skies of culture
countries of cravings
time after time
all lines

have been crossed a sanctuary, we
become
the cross   ing
the flying
the love   ing
a verb in the making
you become free by freeing
all
from its proper cage
its rightful page
break it
cross   it
free it
like you mean it

B

boldly, i swallowed keys
i had no right to
in hopes you'll dare the depths
to find them

come evening
i bury books, many, all
just to watch them sprout secretly
bearing their weight
in ways i dream to

i learned that blooming
is a type of bulbous growing
a type of bubbling becoming
something with a life of its own
a pregnancy induced by sun & sight
and all those hours spent pouring in the dark

you must prepare the body
for dilation of spirit
give birth
become a live being

BLOODY BRILLIANT

i have been kept away from this
my own blood
the power to create worlds.

*cuando lo guardo, lo siento. lo amo. lo agradesco. lo respiro. es la sangre
de mi vida. la poder de dos mil universos, suspienderlos como luces
brillantes en la cara de una mujer. la mujer, la sola mujer, una, ella es
una y todo, yo y ella, la fuerza innocente y destructiva, que te hace florar
y brincar en el mismo tiempo.*

now i come back, crying.
i found god here.
the power of the ocean in a drop,
no longer disillusioned.
now clear. now bold and bloody,
now a wild womb warrior.

this is my blood i've been missing.
years that this fertile fluid
has been thrown in the landfill.
hidden. rolled up. disposed of quickly.

today i collect it
put it on the altar
revered it. prayed with it.
listened.
today i listened to her.
who she is. what she wants.
her power. her prowl.

this blood grows gardens
i cherish it
this blood clears pathways.

this blood senses beyond senses
i own it
this blood triumphs.

this blood howls in the darkness
i hear it
this blood runs free.

this blood builds empires
i feed it
this blood runs me.

this blood is life force
from a cave of constant creativity
adaptivity
exclusivity
whoever comes in
will stay long enough
to be burned away

until the soul remains
until there is only blood
soul and blood

tell me what is in your blood
what lurks, what lingers, what lusts
for life
do you know your blood
do you feel your blood
do you hear your blood
let it speak
let it move, rise, let it
break things
limits

stories
let it roam, cluster, weep
enter the earth, take root
speak with the mother
she will come back to you
she will come back to you
she will be there for you
receive each other

take this blood
water the new earth
be fierce with it
be fiery
be **BLOODY BRILLIANT**
be you, like this
blood-covered
blood-thirsty
blood-smitten
powerful
and free.

VINO: LA SANGRE DE LA TIERRA

take this blood — yours/mine
and do not spill a drop, it says

use it wholly
annointing life, it says

to be fully alive you must know how
and when
to die, it says
that i must keep dying
keep dying fruitfully
each day
like grapes die
to a good wine

and cups will always be full — yours/mine
we'll live intoxicated
and do the magic
we came here for

SOMETHING ELSE

i want your alchemy
the things you turned to water
the oceans that sleep inside you —
i want something else

we came to the edge
we ran from the edge
summoned by the water —
i have been taken over
by something else

look at all the listening that brought us here
to the sand that speaks;
don't look back,

become undone
look, there's a wave
another wave
another way —
and we are turning
into something else

DANCE AS A WAY TO BREAK

dance as a way to break
whatever calcified words live in these bones, break
the patriarchal patterns patrolling this place, dance
as a way to breathe
through that fire, make
lava channel most of its magic
underground, away from the untrained eye,
dance as the last resort
before becoming a tsunami, swallowing sins
dance as a deadly weapon
dance as lifeforce
dance as dreamweaving
as the only resurrection from a life long dead,
the only plague that multiplies behind masks,
it's too late, you've breathed it already so say it with me
i dance like a swallow, free
i dance like the infinite me
i dance to claim what i see
i am the power that be.
dance as the only place to go
without maps
or masks
expecting nothing but
ruins —
rising royally rootfull
remnants of ceremonial circles,
of belonging,
of sanctifying place to person,
purpose to part, remember now?
we offered blessings and became them,
remember how
& say it with me
i am a place made sacred

in the secret bends by
secret hands, i move
with the earth that's how i dance
i grieve with the earth
i shake with the earth that's how i dance
i love with the earth
i break with the earth
i am in ruins each time, i dance
defeated
and that's how i know
dance is the way in and the way out
the way through
the way to lose and the way to win
the way to know
the way to claim
the way to change what moves
and only when i am the dance
i am the way

SEAGLASS

you shine like this too, i know it
between the dark and dawn
when dreams have a hold on you
and you feel infinite
you are what you are
and to be more of it
is what the blue jay insists you do
today more than yesterday
turn blue
oceanwide, skyridden
blue like the flame burning ultimate
blue like the seaglass turned intimate
and polished you clean and true
so you can find your healing
and catch the sun
midflight

LIVE IN THE ANSWER

but the soul wants this
and who am i to say no

the ocean, my love
is calling
aaheeeh-yiiwa

i am running with no feet
into the infinite yes, into
the wave, yes
the depth, yes
the yes of yes

}} take me {{

i live in the leap, i sleep
unafraid, yes

anchored - ancient
fresh - flowing
and if i pause for too long
then my question just wasn't simple enough

there is a right time right place
for all the answers
to turn back into question form
and you begin your life, alive
living as the answer you want to hear

you are the echo coming back
you are the echo coming back

hear that? your soul is singing

~

in this moment
i am free, a whistle
in the wind, in this moment
i am me
a child of the light that comes undone
in the silence, the soft cover
opening
revealing a universe unwritten
the creation of a new story, i am
seeding the pages with verbs
actions of a myth unspoken

in this moment, liberation lives
as steam at the top of my mug
rising true in the bones

in this moment, freedom has me
and i happily let it

you have to get quiet... so quiet that nothing feels missing. a type of quiet where your hands are made of ears and everything you touch is ritual. coffee. tea. there's a ring left behind every cup that is full. that is how life speaks to you. how many languages do you understand?

beyond words, there is so much to talk about. we have a million conversations with everything near and far. i assure you it is better information than you'll ever find on the news. let it in. your gates must be wordless, like the lips of the morning.
only song.
only sense.
only soul.

it's funny, then, that words are the ones that lead us to the wordless. we must get to know them so intimately that we break through to the other side. weave them wisely enough and they'll take us to the edge of a wild canyon, a keyless door, a morning window — some type of opening. it is there that we must continue alone. step into intimacy. into connection. into laughter. into courage. into realization. into bliss. into awakening. into sky. into a filling type of quiet that makes rings around it.

like a good parent, words teach you to eventually leave them.

every good poem leads to the wordless. every good conversation is a poem and moves you beyond where you are. if it is not true and clear-intentioned, raw and time-enduring, then it is not a good conversation. if it does not lead you through the self and beyond it, if it gets stuck somewhere along the way — in identity, in label, in political correctness — then it is a conversation that will never lead home. i don't want to have it.

we were never meant to hold on to words the way we do, building walls that divide and conquer. words as identity, we wear them like they're us. "old", "stressed", "hippie", "non-binary", "immigrant", "entrepreneur", "tired", "spiritual". but words belong to no body. they are just bridges we use, temporary shelter. careful, that you don't make yourself small enough to end where they end.

the sky begins at your feet, did you know? and you, well you begin at the feet of words. words walk in your expanse, hopeful that you pick the right ones to realize it. "i'm going back to the quiet that made me, will you come with?", they say. let's go home to the quiet that endures, the core of the manifest, the universal language. shh, god is asleep in the meadow.

in the beginning was the word, yes... the only tool that is so far from the infinite that only it could lead you back to it.